An

Early

Afterlife

By LINDA PASTAN

A Perfect Circle of Sun
Aspects of Eve
The Five Stages of Grief
Waiting for My Life
PM/AM: New and Selected Poems
A Fraction of Darkness
The Imperfect Paradise
Heroes in Disguise
An Early Afterlife

An
Early
Afterlife

Poems
LINDA PASTAN

W · W · NORTON & COMPANY · NEW YORK · LONDON

Printed in the United States of America

The text of this book is composed in New Caledonia
with the display set in Bulmer.
Composition by ComCom division of Haddon Craftsmen, Inc.
Manufacturing by The Courier Companies, Inc.

Library of Congress Cataloging-in-Publication Data
Pastan, Linda, 1932–
    An early afterlife : poems / Linda Pastan.
       p.   cm.
    I. Title.
    PS3566.A775E27   1995
    811'.54—dc20   94-11268

ISBN 0-393-03727-4

W. W. Norton & Company, Inc., 500 Fifth Avenue, New York, N.Y. 10110
W. W. Norton & Company Ltd., 10 Coptic Street, London WC1A 1PU

1 2 3 4 5 6 7 8 9 0

For Anna

Contents

2. Almost an Elegy   35

Acknowledgments

I would like to thank the following periodicals in which many of these poems first appeared:

The Atlantic Monthly; The Brandeis Review; The Cream City Review; The Gettysburg Review; Harvard Magazine; The Indiana Review; The New Republic; The New Virginia Review; The Paris Review; Pivot; Plum; Poetry; Prairie Schooner; Ruby; The Southern Review; Tikkun; The Threepenny Review; TriQuarterly; The Virginia Quarterly Review, and *Visions International.*

I would also like to thank my editor, Carol Houck Smith, and my agent, Jean Naggar, for their friendship and support. And thanks to Myra Sklarew, Ann Darr, Jean Nordhaus, and Michael Collier for good suggestions about so many of these poems.

1. The Arithmetic
of Alternation

The Python

at the Children's Zoo

The children holding the python
all along its ten-foot mottled body
are like the blind men with the elephant—
what can they know
of what they hold beneath their fingers,
these not quite babies
still in the Eden of preschool,
sloughing off their winter jackets now
in the steamy weather
of the reptile house.

And this creature they dare
to carry, this undulating river
of muscle, supple and curving and
thick as the arm of its keeper,
what does it know of sin
or apples, wanting only to follow the flick
of its two-pronged tongue
(like those blind men following
their tapping canes) to any place
its hunger takes it.

The Lumberjacks

They entered Eden
with their saws and axes,
and as Eve watched
from just beyond the gate
they turned the live trees
into timber, a carnage

of chestnut, cedar, alder,
spilling the fruit and
stripping the bark, measuring,
cutting into four-by-fours and
two-by-sixes—numbering
now instead of naming, until

even the complicitous apple
was felled, and the smell
of sawdust was like death
in the nostrils,
and it was evening
and another day.

Espaliered Pear Trees

You tack the pear trees to the wall
in a mime of crucifixion—
their limbs splayed flat,
their leafed backs toward us—
and water them with a hose.

Last week you called the bonsai
living haiku, paring
its tender branches
as ruthlessly
as you would your nails,

while I could only think
of Chinese women
tottering
on their bound feet.
Here in the garden,

where the cost of beauty
is partly pain, we kneel
on the resilient ground
trying to befriend the soil
we must become.

Long after Eden,
the imagination flourishes
with all its unruly weeds.
I dream of the fleeting
taste of pears.

The Book

In the book of shadows
the first page is dark
and the second darker still,
but on the next page,
and the next, there is a flickering
as if the shadows are dancing
with themselves, as if they are dancing
with the leaves they mimic.
Before Narcissus found the pool
it was his shadow he loved,

the way we grow to love our deaths
when we meet them
in dreams. For as we turn
the pages of the book
each page grows heavier
under our numbed fingers, and only
the shadows themselves
are weightless,
only the shadows welcome us
beneath their cool canopy.

Narcissus at 60

If love hadn't made him clumsy,
if he hadn't fallen forward,
had never drowned
in his own perfection,

what would he have thought
about his aging face
as it altered, year after year
season by season?

In the old conspiracy
between the eye
and its reflection, love casts
a primal shadow.

Perhaps he would blame
the wrinkling surface of the pool
for what he saw
or think the blemishes

on his once smooth cheek
were simply small fish
just beneath the lethal skin
of the water.

At Indian River Inlet

Long before there was light, water
existed, as if chaos itself
had been a kind of rainstorm.

Maybe that's why this landscape seems
so elemental, a place
where blues and greens leak

into each other, where water
and land are married
with all the binding ties of salt.

Today the wind moves
over the flat plain of the cove,
bending the waves

into rows. I could be standing
in a field somewhere
watching

the grass blades bow, regiment
by regiment,
as far as the horizon.

Even the single fisherman
leaning over the side
of his boat

is like some good farmer, seeding
the water with prayers
and curses, setting his bait

with a love based upon hunger,
a skepticism only the faithful
really know.

Our own tides move restlessly
in and out. Color rushes
to our faces, then subsides,

love comes and goes,
tears in their mercy catch
at our reedy lashes. At night

our houses sink
on their foundations
like small boats rocking on their heels,

and over creek and estuary,
field and farm,
over every ambiguity

of darkness
the moon comes, casting
its mended net.

On the Threshold of Silence

When you hear voices, stop awhile
and listen, even if they babble on
like the creek, for instance
with so much winter runoff

the new grass is flattened along its edges.
Listen to the whir of bees
cooling their secret honey;
to the arrogant sounds of a squirrel

hiding its acorns
under a map of fallen leaves.
The pen scratches its way
over the empty paper.

The world is almost enough.
Even the birds speak
in grammatical tongues,
and voices rise

from the burning bush
which we call Winged Euonymus
or float down from a ladder
in the sky whose rungs

are poplar branches climbing
towards the white cornice of cloud,
trying to breach the improbable
ceiling of heaven.

"Ideal City"

oil on panel, Central Italy, c. 1500

Set in the silence of pure perspective,
the ideal city has no people, only buildings.
On these streets order rules with a golden
stylus, and in the balance of dome
and arch and doorframe, we find
serenity, child of proportion.
Maybe this place is an alternate Eden
created by an urban God who hated gardens.
Or maybe this is Heaven just before Judgment Day,
and the buildings are simply waiting for the Chosen
who will rise from their graves to come and inhabit them.
At night when the clarity of light must finally fade
I hope that the Virtues step down from their columns to dance
a little or, better still, cook pasta in the invisible kitchens.

But the Italian clouds with their casual cumulus shapes
don't really belong in this sky, and though the doorways
are partly ajar, they seem to open on nothing but blankness.
In such a city, I wonder where lovers can embrace
or where the dog can lift his shaggy leg.
Then I want to break all the laws of Geometry,
to litter these spotless streets with the pungency
of orange peels and the glaze of cigarette wrappers,
to put my arms around the bronzed columns, then shinny
up them, pretending to be one of the Virtues myself.
I want to run through the streets playing the radio
with its volume turned all the way up.
I want to sign my name, and yours,
with the scarlet graffiti of laughter.

Daylight Savings

I hadn't remembered
it would get dark
so early, or how leaves

like minutes wrenched
from the clock
last spring

would fall invisibly
one by one
this whole gratuitous hour.

It is only five. The chill
in the air becomes
a cold breath

at the ear whispering:
*call in the children, light
the stoves,*

*it is time to live inside
yourselves, in rooms
whose blue-black windows hold*

only your chastened faces.
Even the birds
are leaving,

though the crows remain,
wrapping themselves in the dark
serge of their wings.

Beall Mountain Seasonal

1. Columbus Day

Tentative
as envoys to
an undiscovered
country,
the first leaves
come circling down on
the sweet currents
of Indian summer
air, each leaf
its own
small vessel,
a dozen
colored sails
becoming
an armada.
And soon
the world we know
will disappear
behind us,
and what will be
discovered
is simply
winter.

2. Thanksgiving

like a secret
suddenly disclosed

a deer at the window
fills the morning

with the silence
of grace, mouth

full of delicate
leaves,

and in one blink
straightens its arced back

into a disappearing
arrow

3. The First Day of Winter

How many birds
will disappear
today, taking
their songs with them,

leaving behind
not silence
but the rasping sound
of the wind

honing
its razored edge
along the branches
of trees

the color
of all the autumns
rusted away
already.

The Birds

are heading south, pulled
by a compass in the genes.
They are not fooled
by this odd November summer,
though we stand in our doorways
wearing cotton dresses.
We are watching them

as they swoop and gather—
the shadow of wings
falls over the heart.
When they rustle among
the empty branches, the trees
must think their lost leaves
have come back.

The birds are heading south;
instinct is the oldest story.
They fly over their doubles,
the mute weathervanes,
teaching all of us
with their tailfeathers
the true north.

Camping at the Headlands
of the Rappahannock

We love each landscape
as if it were a part
of our human body,

even the desert
with its waterless beaches;
even the craters of the moon—

those blistered rocks
we christen with the names
of our desire.

Limbs of trees we say,
or foothills,
or bodies of water,

and it is more than metaphor we mean
when we take the river
into our arms.

Requiem

Last year an army
of caterpillars ravished our woods,
their tent cities everywhere,
and Japanese beetles
in their newly plated armor came
for the roses, even as we watched.
Now, riddled with mold
the dogwoods fade out, leaf by heart-
shaped leaf. I remember
the stories of Dutch elms withdrawing
their prodigal gifts of shade.
I remember the seventeen-year locusts,
how we walked, umbrellas raised against
their bodies raining down on us;
how they unraveled the poplars
one stitch at a time.
Though the earth may comfort us
on her voluminous lap, giving
with one flower-filled hand
as she takes away with the other,
I will mourn these milky brides
betrothed to spring, still standing lithe
as girl gymnasts on the grass,
here at the edge of winter.

The Way Things Are

In the last years of the dogwood,
the countdown starting berry
by bright berry,
in the first October
of my seventh decade,
a month when colors run
together, red
into rust into
every kind of amber,
when the leaves make
their metaphysical journey
from one form to another
on tides of air, on the rushing
currents of rain singing
down the ditches, when
the answer to every question
is smoke,
I wake this morning
in the heaviness of flesh
to the throb of a mourning dove
and the wood thrush
with its premonitions
of beauty, to the sun
which is no color
and every color.

With the Passing of the Leaves

The masks are dropping
from the trees,
the small shriveled mouths
stutter in every wind

and fall, a thousand
veils tremble to reveal
the Baptist's head in its
perpetual winter.

I have had nothing
but beauty to shield me
from my neighbors
with their rough

machines, their strife,
and now between
my nakedness
and the world

there will only be thin
rags of snow at the window
and such fierce light
I must shut my eyes

and like the animals
of the field, hibernate
through the marauding
winter.

leaves

1.
a gypsy reads the palm
of a fallen leaf

2.
the rake says: let me gather you together,
let us make smoke

3.
in these patchwork woods
we lie down on the rustling quilt of leaves

4.
sharp as a compass needle, the stem
of a falling leaf spins north

5.
know the parent by the child:
poplar yellow, dogwood red

6.
the willow asks: what color
is regret?

7.
no more than compost ourselves, let us
grow drunk on this sherry-colored weather

8.
the smoke says: I will sting
the nostrils of God

9.
the gypsy says: I see white leaf-shaped flakes come
shivering down, but the future is green

Agoraphobia

"Yesterday the bird of night did sit,
Even at noonday, upon the marketplace,
Hooting and shrieking."
                        —William Shakespeare

1.

Imagine waking
to a scene of snow so new
not even memories
of other snow
can mar its silken
surface. What other innocence
is quite like this,
and who can blame me
for refusing
to violate such whiteness
with the booted cruelty
of tracks?

2.

Though I cannot leave this house,
I have memorized the view
from every window—
23 framed landscapes, containing
each nuance of weather and light.
And I know the measure
of every room, not as a prisoner
pacing a cell
but as the embryo knows
the walls of the womb, free
to swim as its body tells it, to nudge
the softly fleshed walls,
dreading only the moment
of contraction when it will be forced
into the gaudy world.

3.
Sometimes I travel as far
as the last stone
of the path, but
every step,
as in the children's story,
pricks that tender place
on the bottom of the foot,
and like an ebbing tide with all
the obsession of the moon behind it,
I am dragged back.

4.
I have noticed in windy fall
how leaves are torn from the trees,
each leaf waving good-bye to the oak
or the poplar that housed it;
how the moon, pinned
to the very center of the window,
is like a moth wanting only to break in.
What I mean is this house
follows all the laws of lintel and ridgepole,
obeys the commandments of broom
and of needle, custom and grace.
It is not fear that holds me here but passion
and the uncrossable moat of moonlight
outside the bolted doors.

Smoke Screen

I love the many dialects of smoke,
leaf smoke and pipe smoke,
chimney smoke,
the way in spite of gravity
it always rises,
as if it were assembling
in some pungent niche of Heaven.
I used to love the smoke rings
you blew, those insubstantial
lassos of desire
that roped me in.
Now I love wood smoke
and kitchen smoke—the breath of soup
lifting from the pot, contrails
of morning toast, barely burning.
Consider the signals the Indians sent—
that first skywriting,
or how all fires give up the ghost
in veils, in clouds like parachutes
ascending. I love the way
from every household hearth
a genie spirals up a helix
of its own making.
And we walk home, watching
the smoke our breath makes
on the wintry air, not noticing
our days, our nights going slowly
up in smoke.

Meditation at 30,000 Feet

I always knew
the earth loved us
and wanted us back.

Why else would gravity tug
at our limbs with such quiet
persistence?

Why else would the soil open
its dark body, longing
to let us in?

The Suicide

She carried with her
wherever she went
a value-added tax of pain,
like one of those weights

a runner straps
to her legs
to make motion
through space more

deliberate.
And so she moved heavily
through those last
days, mistaking

the horizon
for the finish line,
rewriting the script
of her own life

whose alternative endings
she wouldn't stay here
long enough
to read.

The Soldier's Wife

In these early days of war
I barricade each entrance to my body
against even the dream
of invasion, burn
the bridges so carefully built
between us, hunker down
as if for endless winter, shivering
in this new armor of gooseflesh.

The starlings with their gift
for mimicry screech
outside my locked window,
or is it merely music
misunderstood? Tonight, even the flesh
of fruit bruises easily, and earthquake
or tidal wave, some natural disaster,
would seem nearly benign.

It is that odd chromosome,
the unleashed bliss of anger I saw
in his eyes as he left,
that makes my ring finger twitch
in its gold shackle and my mouth
form not a smile, not even a frown
but a crevice; a refusal; an armed border
bristling with teeth.

Stationary Bicycle

You pedal furiously
into a future you're trying
hard to prolong
by this exercise,
though the landscape
that rolls by here is time
passing, with its lists
of things undone
or not done properly,
and all this effort,
the fierce monotony
of this ride feels
much like life itself—
going nowhere
strenuously,
redeemed in part
by the imagination, its trance
of rivers and trees,
its shady roads unwinding
just beyond your closed eyes,
or even on the tv screen
you sometimes watch
as you ride, mile
after mile of drama
unfolding while you pump
and pump, proceeding
from here to here
at twenty theoretical
miles per hour, your legs
beginning to throb, as if
the body communicates
in a code of pain, saying
never mind the future,
you're here right now, alive.

Baseball

When you tried to tell me
baseball was a metaphor

for life: the long, dusty travail
around the bases, for instance,

to try to go home again;
the Sacrifice for which you win

approval but not applause;
the way the light closes down

in the last days of the season—
I didn't believe you.

It's just a way of passing
the time, I said.

And you said: that's it.
Yes.

Surfeit

There are so many poems
in the world. There are so many
tea-colored peaches ripening
or rotting on the trees;
there is so much noisy
birdsong, so many trees.
I long for the God of abstinence
whose single fruit
is the sun, whose brief hymn
is the one poem necessary.

Calling

When the word calls, you follow
even in the kitchen proofing yeast for bread—
a different kind of rising.

Or if you're in bed and halfway
from the shore of wakefulness already,
still you must swim back, arm over heavy arm

to where full consciousness waits
with its honed pencil.
For whether or not you want it,

whether or not you're ready, you must
grasp it now in your good right hand
as if it alone can save you.

Ruins

We picnic by these bleached ruins
a few miles from the village
where we bought this rough
bread and cheese, this bottle
of wine shaped
like a Cycladic goddess.
Nearby is Homer's Aegean
where bathers in their sculpted
flesh, their beauty, might have been
the models for the limbs
now broken, the faces
fallen from the frieze
of this temple whose ruins
we love because they show
how life is both continuous
and brief and must
be honored with good wine,
with bread and cheese.

The English Novel

In The English Novel, where I spent my girlhood,
I used to think chilblains were a kind of biscuit,
and everything was always pearled with fog—
the moors with their purpling heather
and the beveled windows where the heroines,
my sisters, waited for heroes
who would find them eventually, after one or both
threaded their way through some kind of moral
labyrinth, shadowed and thorny. He was worth waiting for,
and anyway the slowness of the clocks was deliberate
as if minutes, like pence, had different meanings then.
There was no polyester. Everything was brocade and velvet,
even the landscapes, those hills embroidered
with flowers, and though sex was hardly mentioned
it was clearly a scent in the air like the sachets
in the cupboards, subtle but pervasive as the smell
of lavender or viburnum or tallow from all the smoky,
snuffed-out candles. Furniture and forests, marriages
were eternal then, and though there was always a plot
it hardly mattered. As for too much coincidence,
doesn't the moon always wander through the sky at the exact
moment the lovers are wandering through the park, even
        today,
even in this city with its fake Victorian façades?
And all the familiar faces we notice at the movies
or across a restaurant, couldn't they be our half brothers
or cousins, lost once in the deep and mysterious gene pool—
descendants, some of them, of Emma and Mr. Knightley,
or the ones with Russian faces descended from Ladislaw
        maybe,
who could have come from a place just a few hours by carriage
from the shtetl where my great-great-grandmother
somehow acquired her blond hair and blue blue eyes?

the arithmetic of alternation

today I write
of the shadows
flowers make
on a white wall,
the texture of petals
and leaves like a flat braille,
a brightness
even without color

but tomorrow
I will tell
how on the warmest day
there is an icy edge
to things, a darkness
at the rim
of every shining
object

this is the arithmetic
of alternation,
the way the hours,
the seasons
arrange themselves,
it keeps us honest,
it keeps us turning
the page

2. Almost an Elegy

Memory

As stealthy
as a winter deer
moving among
tree trunks
and as hungry . . .

Look! the white
flick of a tail
as if the moon
had suddenly been
uncovered.

Silent Treatment

On still nights, I think
the leaves must listen
for the smallest breeze, as I do—
the marriage of sound
and touch.

In this quiet house,
there is only the buzz
of electrons through the wires
to comfort me, the moan
of water deep in pipes.

In winter I watch
the snow muffled
in whiteness as it falls.
I see the moon move mutely
from phase to phase.

We replicate our childhoods
despite ourselves,
those years when
the covers of a book
screened out

the audible world;
when my father, clearing
his throat of language,
punished me again
with silence.

The Bronx, 1942

When I told him to shut up,
my father slammed the brakes and left
me like a parcel in the car
on a strange street, to punish me
he said for lack of respect, though
what he always feared was lack of love.
I know now just how long

forgiveness can take
and that it can be harder than respect,
or even love. My father stayed angry
for a week. But I still remember
the gritty color of the sky through
that windshield and how, like a parcel,
I started to come apart.

Courbet's "Still Life with Apples and Pomegranate"

To lift himself from one of his depressions,
my father took up painting, oil on canvas
for which he had no teacher,
just an apprenticeship in sheer will
and bagfuls of groceries to practice on.

I can still smell those apples, and sometimes peaches,
going slyly to rot on my mother's velvet shawl
whose blue folds he slowly re-created
one by one by one as if they were waves
on an artificial ocean.

Courbet's fruit have so much roundness,
such warmth and homeliness beside the pewter tankard,
you could almost say they had humanity,
if apples could be human.
And as I stand in this crowded museum,

all these years after my father's death,
they make me grieve for him
and his precise, mistaken apples,
not for his failures;
for how stubbornly he tried.

Poetry Reading

Your words are like the knife
in the hand of my surgeon father
whose completed face was hidden
from me by that green mask,
whose eyes were so focused
he could see every organ,
every arterial river laid out
before him—a map of the world
for him to choose from.
And though that knife could kill
as well as heal, still I was willing
to lie down, belly up, like a young wolf
before the alpha dog, trusting him
with my defenseless life.

MD 67

I am riding
the moving stairway
from the dark
caves of
Pennsylvania
Station up
to the granite noise
and flash of New
York City, still
expecting to see
my father (angel
with only the curves
of a mustache for
wings) waiting
at the curb
in his finned
Chrysler,
having run
the stoplight from
the next world
back to this.

Landscape with Statues

Sometimes the journeys
we accomplish in sleep
deliver us here, open-eyed
on a spring morning,
the only debris
the dogwood petals
that litter the stony paths
with pale confetti.

This is our fertile crescent,
a place of winged flowers
and stemmed birds, whose names
we sometimes remember
and sometimes invent.
In this landscape the rivers
are swollen with longing,
and we wade in them.

In this landscape our losses
are nearly recovered, for the dead
come back to us
in all their old poses,
as if they were playing
the childhood game of statues
on lawns so green they drink
the shadows to oblivion.

Because I was never a child

I never grew up,
and though what I glimpsed
in the other room I didn't understand,
I knew as well as I know now
that the dark flowers in that room
were composed of shadows.

I knew even in the crib, frightened
by dust motes swirling in planetary light
that danger is odorless—as pervasive
as air, and the nightlight
is a worthless charm
against darkness.

I grow more childlike now.
Sometimes I trust in the future,
believing babies are innocent, despite
their old men's faces,
their obsessive teeth.
On winter evenings I walk

the windy sidewalks, clicking
my castanet heels, hardly noticing
how the flickering tongue of the stranger
flares like a ruined candle,
making unruly shadows
in the closed room of the dark.

Family Ties

Bound at ankles
and wrists,
see how helpless

we are, heart-
strings plucked
pizzicato

by what our mothers said,
what our daughters
fail to say.

And all the old clichés roused
from their sleep
turn back

into metaphor—time flies:
a Florentine hourglass
with wings, here

in the arena of the family,
where everybody loses,
everybody wins.

Almost an Elegy

1. Keeping Watch

You have always lived in the shadows cast
by other lives, happy to be almost invisible—
the obedient child, typecast in your mother's life;
the mother in a new play starring children,
their pure insistence, the flame of their mortality
keeping you at a rolling boil.

It was the future you lived in,
as now you inhabit the past, and the two
have the same indeterminate sky,
brilliantly cloudless, the same
shifting walls between which
you place invented furniture.

So little changes. The Ferris wheel of months
revolves continuously, a ride you take
over and over, locked in the view:
December whiteouts; another April; May
weighted with flowers; November's leafy rags
in which you wrap yourself.

It is enough to bear witness, to finger the secrets
you have always kept like extra buttons:
the baby's milky face, a rage of orchids,
the rough, particular sounds of love—
clues the senses give you to gifts withheld so long
you wouldn't recognize them.

2. Recessional

You are taking up
less space in the world,
giving bits of yourself away—
a chapter here,
crochet work there,

making of your own life
a charity
for the indifferent
to pick over,
to discard or to keep.

You are becoming
transparent—a pane
of antiqued glass
flawed perhaps, though
you don't break.

You are a secret
whispered once
from mouth to ear
that nobody bothers
to tell.

3. Letting Go

For you, newly mortal, there is one
question left: how to leave
this world whose apron strings
of light tug at you
at the first hint of departure,

tie you to the things
you almost forgot to love:
the fruit tamed in the hand;
a child carelessly climbing
the ladder of generations;

seascapes and dogwoods
and seasons. Though
animals know nothing
of their deaths, the black
bear lumbers harshly

into darkness,
and whole tribes
of starlings scatter
like buckshot at the hunter's
soft approach.

Fear and its long shadow
are also of this world, and regret
is only the underside of longing.
If you close your eyes, the first blade
of grass has not been invented yet,

and light will wait
with perfect patience
for the eyelid
to be raised again . . .
and slowly lowered.

The Recovery Zone

If I could befriend this pain,
could consider the wracking
of the spirit
a kind of exercise,

if I could see myself
in pure perspective: no more
than a comma in the long epic
of suffering,

then I would slake my thirst
with these salty tears
and decorate my pale body
with love's bloody stigmata.

High Summer

The earth smells of flowers
and corruption—so many
shades of green
that caterpillar and leaf
are indistinguishable,
even as one obliterates
the other.

Aunt Ruth sits
on the back porch, rocking
towards her death.
The smallest cousin swims
into the future. Look
at the water, so beautiful
in all that it conceals.

In a Northern Country

Yesterday in a northern country
my last aunt died, taking
my maiden name with her into silence,
and there is no one left
who knew her here
for me to tell.

I am tired of the litany
of months, September . . . October . . .
I am tired of the way the seasons
keep changing, mimicking
the seasons of the flesh
which are real and finite.

The world wounds us
with its beauty, as if it knew
we had to leave it soon.
She must have watched
the deep Canadian lake she loved
sheathe itself in early ice,

the few last leaves
on the birch tree tremble
like half notes, vibrato
outside her sickroom window
until November came
with its winds and took them.

April Again

April again,
the funeral month, heaping
its flowers everywhere.

Outside the window that was yours
the star magnolia blooms
in its leafless firmament.

It was an easy month to die in,
the ground hospitable to any planting.
Six full years. Is it possible

that every time I think of you
you know it and are keeping track?
Love is always incomplete,

distracted, not enough.
And though I've gone on
with my life

beneath the lucky surface
of the everyday,
tectonic plates of earth,

like squares of your polished
linoleum, shift again
under my feet.

Ghosts

My lovely ghosts are unaware
of boundaries. They step from my dreams
into the early morning air
as if they were offering
breakfast, the way they used to.

They have my sculpted cheekbones,
my severe hair. At dusk
I see them reflected
in the darkening windows
beyond which, like static

from a distant transmission,
the bitter snow is starting to fall.
Oh my lovely ghosts,
when I speak your names aloud
I think you forgive me.

Old Photograph Album

These pages, crumbling under my fingers
as I turn them, chronicle the lives
of the people I loved, years before
I was there to love them. Mother.
Great-aunts and cousins. Here are their naked
infancies on sheepskin rugs; their exodus
across decades of childhood and youth;
the shy solemnity of their weddings.
In the old country my father in knickers
clowns and spends his foreign dollars
on his last visit before that country
closes down. The Adirondacks.
The Catskills. New York—its pushcarts,
its ancient children—more foreign
to me than the streets of Troy or Rome.
The glue loosens under the small black
triangles that hold the pictures in place,
reminding me of those torn
pieces of mourning ribbon pinned
to our blouses or coats at funerals.
Here are the people I have lost
because I can't believe in the green
pastureland of hymns or in the haloed
faces of angels, outlined
in golden threads on altar cloths:
Grandma and Grandpa,
Ada and Ruth. If only I thought
we would meet just one more time
even in purgatory, that anteroom
to someone else's heaven, with its horsehair sofas
and shabby twenties furniture, peopled
with ghosts in high starched collars and velvet hats.

The Laws of Primogeniture

My grandson has my father's mouth
with its salty sayings
and my grandfather's crooked ear
that heard the soldiers coming.

He has the pale eyes of the Cossack
who saw my great-great-grandmother
in the woods, then wouldn't stop
looking.

And see him now, pushing
his bright red fire truck towards
a future he thinks he's inventing
all by himself.

What We Fear Most

for R after the accident

We have been saved one more time
from what we fear most.
Let us remember this moment.
Let us forget it if we can.
Just now a kind of golden dust
settles over everything:
the tree outside the window,
though it is not fall;
the cracked sugar bowl,
so carefully mended once.
This light is not redemption,
just the silt of afternoon sun
on an ordinary day,
unlike any other.

Flowers

Someone I love is getting married,
and I am composing poems about flowers, hyacinths
and lilacs, as if there were something
intrinsically bridal about these outgrowths of the plant
flaunting itself, attracting insects and birds
to the exact and fragrant place of pollen.

And someone I love is dying.
Flowers will be wanted for her too,
lilies perhaps, though all that is required
is a handful of good dirt on a plain pine box,
and all the funeral bouquets will be sent
to a hospital somewhere, where the sick will wake

one morning to a confusion of scents.
I wonder, partly in innocence,
why everything seems to mean something else,
and I marvel at how we comfort
ourselves and each other with the fragile
symptoms of beauty, with petals

of roses for love, with snowdrops for hope,
whether we are setting out on a journey
or simply waving good-bye from the dock
as the ship pulls out and a wake of tossed flowers
floats for a little while, delicate as foam
on the water, before it disappears.

Gladiola

In noisy shades of
apricot and pink
the blossoms

of the gladiola open
all down the long aisle
of the stem

like a choral procession
or the woody
notes

of a flute
opening one stop
at a time.

Wisteria Floribunda

Half drunk
on the heavy scent
of purple,

I almost expect
the naked
trees

to step from behind
their fringed
and beaded

curtains,
to the electric thrum
of bees.

Snow Showers: a Prothalamion

for Rachel and David

You are teaching my daughter the language
of the stars, the whole sky
glazed with them in freezing Wisconsin,
and both your faces tilted up
as though you were reading, were trying
to learn by heart the night's
illuminated pages. I picture her
putting her eye to a telescope and seeing
her first close-up
of what I still call the heavens.
It must have been like seeing a man's face (yours)
stubbled and cratered, an eyelash length away.
She was a most inventive child.
Now she gives the spin of reality
to her made-up worlds,

while you, fledgling astronomer,
make real worlds, with their long itineraries of light,
seem touched with phantasy.
I want to tell you both how a moment ago
there were snow showers here,
though the sun is back now, and the grass
remains a frozen, spiky green.
But just a moment ago the sky seemed to release
entire galaxies, and stars or star-shaped flakes,
whatever that charged and bridal whiteness was,
swarmed at the windows
until the real and the imagined
became one, a perfect marriage
of opposites, like mine has been.
Come spring, like yours.

Cosmic Dust

for David

On nights when you can't sleep
I think you open the door
to the sky

and taking out a small broom
sweep the cosmic dust
into tidy piles

and label them
with phosphorescent ink
from the nearest moon.

Therefore the morning sky
is nothing if not pure
blue. Therefore you sleep

past noon so the telltale dust
caught in your eye
won't give you away.

Vermilion

Pierre Bonnard would enter
the museum with a tube of paint
in his pocket and a sable brush.
Then violating the sanctity
of one of his own frames
he'd add a stroke of vermilion
to the skin of a flower.
Just so I stopped you
at the door this morning
and licking my index finger, removed
an invisible crumb
from your vermilion mouth. As if
at the ritual moment of departure
I had to show you still belonged to me.
As if revision were
the purest form of love.

Ah Love,

you expert
knifethrower, outlining my body

with your gleaming blades
as I stand trembling here

against the bedroom wall.
I was distracted

for months by the color
of your flowers,

by all your flowery
words, for where you come from

it is always tropical.
Now I am ready for you

to do your worst. Look,
I am opening my blouse—here

is my uncovered heart.
Just aim for it.

Foreshadowing

is what writers call it, meaning
Chekhov's famous pistol
which must go off in the final act;
or how an aging poet used melancholy
as the alphabet of childhood.

It is the hint God gave us
when He invented night
on the first page of creation—
a recurring darkness over Eden
long before the fall.

It is one red leaf in August;
a wrinkled newborn's
sharp, protesting cry.
I remember our first kiss, the way
it went on and on as if we knew

to separate even once would be dangerous,
would foreshadow a final
parting, real as a gunshot
which, mouth against mouth,
we could deny.

The Password

It is simply a question
of syllables,
a word

the smallest
child may
know.

But when I say it
the sentry in you
smiles,

and all the doors fly open
on their winged
hinges.

The Apple Shrine

Last week you gathered armfuls of apple blossoms
from trees along the roadway, and a few
from the bent Cortland down the street
to place beneath our nameless apple tree
for pollination, you said, so we'd have fruit
next winter. Looking out the window at those rags
and shreds of blossoms beneath the tree,
it could have been a makeshift shrine I saw
in one of those unlikely places where miracles
are said to happen, sightings of angels
or the Virgin, where later ordinary people
place gifts of dolls and colored handkerchiefs.
How fitting, I thought, as if we worshiped
the garden itself, or spring. Just one day later
and equally strange, but fearful

you seemed to lose your vision, went half blind
after work in the garden, for a transgression
not even you with your Science understand.
Healing too is mysterious, the way the seasons
heal each other, one month at a time;
or what can happen in a week in a darkened room
where we both sat thinking about how quickly
everything can change, how thin the crust
of ice we walk on—such thoughts themselves perhaps
a kind of prayer. Today you start to see again,
and I wonder how long we'll remember to be grateful
before we lose ourselves complicitously
in the everyday, waking up surprised one morning
next autumn when for the first time
our tree will be strung with a rosary of apples.

Hardwood

Do these gnarled and twisted trees
feel greenness surge
at their roots the way saplings do?
When a new leaf breaks through
are they astonished,
as Sarah must have been,
at such an improbable birth?

The woodpecker, with its
firing squad rat-tat-tat, knows
each vulnerable spot on the wrinkled bark.
In a month these trees will resurrect
a shade to sit beneath.
There are stumps
to rest on everywhere.

Migraine

Ambushed by
pins and needles
of light . . . by jagged

voices . . . strobes . . .
the sanctuary is taken
from within.

I am betrayed by
the fractured
senses. I

crouch on the
tilting floor of
consciousness, fearing

the eggshell
skull won't hold, will crack,
as the lid is tightened

another implacable
inch. I would banish every
blessing—these shooting

stars . . . the future . . .
all brilliant
excitations—just for

silence or sleep
or the cotton wool
of the perfected dark.

Flash Forward

Remember those old movies
when the screen was filled with
calendar pages, blowing
away on the breeze
from some studio wind machine,
and we knew that months
had passed, years maybe?

That's how it feels right now
when I look out and see
the leaves blowing
like pages torn
from the November trees,
and I understand suddenly
how old I am.

Mercy

Perhaps our aging eyesight fails
simply because it's easier not to see
what has become of our faces
in the mirrors or in the dark windows
of early winter where we gaze through
our reflections into the cold.
Perhaps that's the reason memory

fails too, a kind of mercy,
as if what we came to the kitchen for
(an aspirin? milk?) isn't as crucial
as just standing there trying to remember
but remembering instead the milky mouths
of childhood, the perfect eyesight
which saw nothing dangerous ahead.

Sometimes

from the periphery
of the family
where I sit watching
my children and
my children's children
in all their bright
cacophony,

I seem to leave
my body—
plump effigy
of a woman, upright
on a chair—
and as I float
willingly away

toward the chill
silence of my own future,
their voices break
into the syllables
of strangers, to whom
with this real hand
I wave good-bye.

An Early Afterlife

". . . a wise man in time of peace, shall make the necessary preparations for war."

—Horace

Why don't we say good-bye right now
in the fallacy of perfect health
before whatever is going to happen
happens. We could perfect our parting,
like those characters in *On the Beach*
who said farewell in the shadow
of the bomb as we sat watching,
young and holding hands at the movies.
We could use the loving words
we otherwise might not have time to say.
We could hold each other for hours
in a quintessential dress rehearsal.

Then we would just continue
for however many years were left.
The ragged things that are coming next—
arteries closing like rivers silting over
or rampant cells stampeding us to the exit—
would be like postscripts to our lives
and wouldn't matter. And we would bask
in an early afterlife of ordinary days,
impervious to the inclement weather
already in our long-range forecast.
Nothing could touch us. We'd never
have to say good-bye again.